DISNEY
THE MUPPETS
MAD LIBS®

by Kendra Levin

PSS!
PRICE STERN SLOAN
An Imprint of Penguin Random House

PRICE STERN SLOAN
Penguin Young Readers Group
An Imprint of Penguin Random House LLC

Mad Libs format copyright © 2016 by Price Stern Sloan,
an imprint of Penguin Random House LLC. All rights reserved.

Concept created by Roger Price & Leonard Stern

© Disney 2016

Published by Price Stern Sloan,
an imprint of Penguin Random House LLC,
345 Hudson Street, New York, New York 10014.
Printed in the USA.

ISBN 9780399542749

1 3 5 7 9 10 8 6 4 2

MAD LIBS

INSTRUCTIONS

MAD LIBS® is a game for people who don't like games! It can be played by one, two, three, four, or forty.

• RIDICULOUSLY SIMPLE DIRECTIONS

In this tablet you will find stories containing blank spaces where words are left out. One player, the READER, selects one of these stories. The READER does not tell anyone what the story is about. Instead, he/she asks the other players, the WRITERS, to give him/her words. These words are used to fill in the blank spaces in the story.

• TO PLAY

The READER asks each WRITER in turn to call out a word—an adjective or a noun or whatever the space calls for—and uses them to fill in the blank spaces in the story. The result is a MAD LIBS® game.

When the READER then reads the completed MAD LIBS® game to the other players, they will discover that they have written a story that is fantastic, screamingly funny, shocking, silly, crazy, or just plain dumb—depending upon which words each WRITER called out.

• EXAMPLE (Before and After)

"_____!" he said _____
      EXCLAMATION   ADVERB

as he jumped into his convertible _____ and
                                            NOUN

drove off with his _____ wife.
                    ADJECTIVE

"_____OUCH_____!" he said _____STUPIDLY_____
      EXCLAMATION   ADVERB

as he jumped into his convertible _____CAT_____ and
                                            NOUN

drove off with his _____BRAVE_____ wife.
                    ADJECTIVE

In case you have forgotten what adjectives, adverbs, nouns, and verbs are, here is a quick review:

An ADJECTIVE describes something or somebody. *Lumpy, soft, ugly, messy,* and *short* are adjectives.

An ADVERB tells how something is done. It modifies a verb and usually ends in "ly." *Modestly, stupidly, greedily,* and *carefully* are adverbs.

A NOUN is the name of a person, place, or thing. *Sidewalk, umbrella, bridle, bathtub,* and *nose* are nouns.

A VERB is an action word. *Run, pitch, jump,* and *swim* are verbs. Put the verbs in past tense if the directions say PAST TENSE. *Ran, pitched, jumped,* and *swam* are verbs in the past tense.

When we ask for A PLACE, we mean any sort of place: a country or city (*Spain, Cleveland*) or a room (*bathroom, kitchen*).

An EXCLAMATION or SILLY WORD is any sort of funny sound, gasp, grunt, or outcry, like *Wow!, Ouch!, Whomp!, Ick!,* and *Gadzooks!*

When we ask for specific words, like a NUMBER, a COLOR, an ANIMAL, or a PART OF THE BODY, we mean a word that is one of those things, like *seven, blue, horse,* or *head.*

When we ask for a PLURAL, it means more than one. For example, *cat* pluralized is *cats.*

MAD LIBS® is fun to play with friends, but you can also play it by yourself! To begin with, DO NOT look at the story on the page below. Fill in the blanks on this page with the words called for. Then, using the words you have selected, fill in the blank spaces in the story.

Now you've created your own hilarious MAD LIBS® game!

WELCOME!

ADJECTIVE _____

ADJECTIVE _____

CELEBRITY _____

PERSON IN ROOM _____

VERB _____

VERB _____

ADJECTIVE _____

ADJECTIVE _____

ADVERB _____

COLOR _____

ADJECTIVE _____

VERB ENDING IN "ING" _____

PLURAL NOUN _____

VERB _____

VERB ENDING IN "ING" _____

PLURAL NOUN _____

VERB _____

MAD LIBS®

WELCOME !

Hi ho, Kermit the Frog here! Welcome to this __wacky__ book
_____ ADJECTIVE

of Muppet Mad Libs! Maybe you know us from our __yucky__
_____ ADJECTIVE

television show or from our movies, featuring stars like __Henrik Lundqvist__
_____ CELEBRITY

and __Ollie__. Or maybe this is the first time you're getting
_____ PERSON IN ROOM

to __swim__ us face-to-face. I think you'll love us, but at the
_____ VERB

very least you'll definitely __smack__ us. And I guarantee we'll
_____ VERB

show you a/an __lumpy__ time! In my time with the Muppets,
_____ ADJECTIVE

I've learned many __jiggy__ lessons. Here are a few I want to
_____ ADJECTIVE

__awkwardly__ share with you:
_____ ADVERB

1. It's not easy being __maroon__.
_____ COLOR

2. It's also not easy to manage a bunch of __funny__ Muppets.
_____ ADJECTIVE

3. If you ever see Miss Piggy __Churtling__ toward
_____ VERB ENDING IN "ING"

   you and she's knocking over all the __floves__ in the
   _____ PLURAL NOUN

   building, there's only one thing to do— __jump__!
   _____ VERB

Now let's get things started . . . Hey, wait a minute—is that Miss Piggy?

Why is she __swimming__ over all those __stink morts__?
_____ VERB ENDING IN "ING"   _____ PLURAL NOUN

Uh-oh! Time for me to __quidh__!
_____ VERB

From THE MUPPETS MAD LIBS® • Copyright © 2016 Disney. Published by Price Stern Sloan, an imprint of
Penguin Random House LLC, 345 Hudson Street, New York, NY 10014.

MAD LIBS® is fun to play with friends, but you can also play it by yourself! To begin with, DO NOT look at the story on the page below. Fill in the blanks on this page with the words called for. Then, using the words you have selected, fill in the blank spaces in the story.

Now you've created your own hilarious MAD LIBS® game!

MISS PIGGY'S MORE OFFICIAL WELCOME

NOUN _____

ADJECTIVE _____

NOUN _____

PLURAL NOUN _____

ADJECTIVE _____

NUMBER _____

PLURAL NOUN _____

VERB _____

ADJECTIVE _____

A PLACE _____

NUMBER _____

ADJECTIVE _____

TYPE OF FOOD _____

Hello, you adorable little __avalanche__, you! Thank *vous* so much
NOUN

for picking up the most ____white____ book ever written, all about
ADJECTIVE

moi: *Miss Piggy's Mad Libs*! As an international film and television

____dumbo____, not to mention a supermodel, fashion icon, and
NOUN

spokespig for my own line of designer ____tree____, *moi* is in
PLURAL NOUN

constant demand. Members of the press are always hounding me—

"What's your secret, Miss Piggy? How do you stay so __fat__?"
ADJECTIVE

It's true that __567__ world leaders and __sharks__
NUMBER   PLURAL NOUN

have fallen in love with me. Just last year, Paris Fashion Week had

to be rescheduled because I had an appointment to __kill__
VERB

that I simply couldn't change. But deep down, I'm still the same

____bumpy____ pig I was when I won my first beauty contest at (the)
ADJECTIVE

____filtyu____ County Fair __467542__ years ago. I was fabulous
A PLACE   NUMBER

then, and I'm fabulous now! Why, you might even describe *moi* as

____orange____. Now, if *vous* will excuse *moi*, my schedule is simply
ADJECTIVE

packed today. For starters, there's some chocolate __broccoli__ in
TYPE OF FOOD

my dressing room that needs my immediate attention.

MAD LIBS® is fun to play with friends, but you can also play it by yourself! To begin with, DO NOT look at the story on the page below. Fill in the blanks on this page with the words called for. Then, using the words you have selected, fill in the blank spaces in the story.

Now you've created your own hilarious MAD LIBS® game!

FOZZIE BEAR'S COMEDY SHOW

PART OF THE BODY (PLURAL) _____

ADJECTIVE _____

TYPE OF FOOD (PLURAL) _____

ARTICLE OF CLOTHING (PLURAL) _____

ADJECTIVE _____

ADJECTIVE _____

ADJECTIVE _____

A PLACE _____

ANIMAL _____

ADJECTIVE _____

ADJECTIVE _____

ADJECTIVE _____

MAD LIBS®
FOZZIE BEAR'S
COMEDY SHOW

Hiya, hiya, hiya! It's me, Fozzie Bear! I just flew in from the coast, and boy

are my ___eyes kdetin___ tired. Ahhh! Funn-eee! But seriously,
PART OF THE BODY (PLURAL)

it's great to be here. The life of a comedian can be ___rasl ty___,
ADJECTIVE

but you fans are what keep me going. Without the tomatoes and

___old carrots___ thrown at me during my act, I'd be starving!
TYPE OF FOOD (PLURAL)

Wocka! Wocka! Now hold on to your ___jeans___,
ARTICLE OF CLOTHING (PLURAL)

because I'm going to tell you the world's funniest joke. Are you ready?

You are going to love this ___purple___ joke! I envy you—I wish I
ADJECTIVE

could hear this joke for the first time. It's that funny. I just hope I have

time to tell it before the ___rocity___ manager of this ___scorchy___
ADJECTIVE   ADJECTIVE

club gives me the hook. Okay, here goes. Did you hear the one about

the kangaroo who walks into (the) ___Tumpa Bay___? ___Lynx___
A PLACE   ANIMAL

comes up to the kangaroo and says, "Hey, I heard that your

___sunny___ baby is so lazy, they call him a pouch potato!" Ahhh!
ADJECTIVE

Wocka! Wocka! Uh-oh, better go. Here comes the ___yummy___
ADJECTIVE

manager with the hook, and the audience is throwing tomatoes. Mmm!

They're juicy and ___rotten___!
ADJECTIVE

MAD LIBS® is fun to play with friends, but you can also play it by yourself! To begin with, DO NOT look at the story on the page below. Fill in the blanks on this page with the words called for. Then, using the words you have selected, fill in the blank spaces in the story.

Now you've created your own hilarious MAD LIBS® game!

KERMIT THE FROG AND FOZZIE BEAR'S ROAD TRIP

ADJECTIVE _____

A PLACE _____

NOUN _____

ADJECTIVE _____

NOUN _____

ADJECTIVE _____

ADJECTIVE _____

ADVERB _____

ADJECTIVE _____

ADJECTIVE _____

NOUN _____

ADJECTIVE _____

PART OF THE BODY (PLURAL) _____

ADVERB _____

ADJECTIVE _____

MAD LIBS
KERMIT THE FROG AND
FOZZIE BEAR'S ROAD TRIP

Long ago, Kermit the Frog lived in a/an _Silky_ swamp not
                                         ADJECTIVE

far from (the) _Siberia_. He sang songs, ate flies, and played
                A PLACE

music on his _bass drum_. One day, a big, fancy agent came to
              NOUN

the swamp and told Kermit he would make a great star. So, Kermit

hopped onto his bicycle and rode off in search of adventure. Moving

right along, the frog wandered into the El Sleezo Cafe, the most

Spiky , meanest, and vilest _chicken_ hole on the face of
ADJECTIVE   NOUN

the earth. Onstage, Fozzie Bear was doing his _awkward_ routine.
                                              ADJECTIVE

With Kermit's help, Fozzie escaped the _silly_ crowd, and the
                                       ADJECTIVE

two took off _blindly_ in Fozzie's _dirty_ Studebaker.
            ADVERB   ADJECTIVE

Kermit and Fozzie became _horible_ friends and decided it was
                         ADJECTIVE

Hollywood or _Everglade_! Along the way they got lost, crashed,
             NOUN

and were chased by a/an _crackly_ restaurant owner who
                        ADJECTIVE

wanted Kermit to be in commercials for his specialty—crispy frog

lungs . But they also made friends that would last a
PART OF THE BODY (PLURAL)

lifetime, and they all lived _silently_ ever after in Hollywood . . .
                             ADVERB

at least, until the next _stinky_ Muppet adventure.
                         ADJECTIVE

MAD LIBS® is fun to play with friends, but you can also play it by yourself! To begin with, DO NOT look at the story on the page below. Fill in the blanks on this page with the words called for. Then, using the words you have selected, fill in the blank spaces in the story.

Now you've created your own hilarious MAD LIBS® game!

KERMIT THE FROG
AND MISS PIGGY

ADJECTIVE _____

NOUN _____

PLURAL NOUN _____

ADJECTIVE _____

PART OF THE BODY (PLURAL) _____

NUMBER _____

NOUN _____

NOUN _____

ADJECTIVE _____

VERB _____

NOUN _____

NOUN _____

PLURAL NOUN _____

PART OF THE BODY (PLURAL) _____

SAME PART OF THE BODY (PLURAL) ____

MAD LIBS®
KERMIT THE FROG
AND MISS PIGGY

The story of Kermit the Frog and Miss Piggy's relationship is a long

and _____stilly_____ one. It all began when Miss Piggy was just a young
       ADJECTIVE

_____varia_____, and Kermit was driving across the country in search
   NOUN

of fame and _____apples_____. When they met, the two shared a very
              PLURAL NOUN

romantic and _____dumb_____ dinner. As they gazed into each other's
               ADJECTIVE

_____arteries_____, it was obvious that theirs was a love that
PART OF THE BODY (PLURAL)

would last for all time, or at least until Miss Piggy got an important

phone call. For _____407.99_____ years, through thick and thin, through
                 NUMBER

_____chalk_____ and _____eraser_____, the pig and the frog have been
   NOUN   **NOUN**

together. Their relationship has always inspired many _____body_____
                                                        ADJECTIVE

questions: Will they be together or _____till_____ once and for all?
                                      VERB

Are they ever going to tie the _____theater_____? Both Kermit and Miss
                                 NOUN

Piggy have dated others, and each time it seems like their relationship

is finally at the end of its _____chair_____. But somehow, against all
                              NOUN

_____twins_____, they always seem to find their way back into each
PLURAL NOUN

other's _____fingernails_____ . . . or at least in the vicinity of each
         PART OF THE BODY (PLURAL)

other's _____fingernails_____.
         SAME PART OF THE BODY (PLURAL)

MAD LIBS® is fun to play with friends, but you can also play it by yourself! To begin with, DO NOT look at the story on the page below. Fill in the blanks on this page with the words called for. Then, using the words you have selected, fill in the blank spaces in the story.

Now you've created your own hilarious MAD LIBS® game!

LADIES AND GENTLEMEN, THE GREAT GONZO!

ADJECTIVE _____

ADJECTIVE _____

NOUN _____

PERSON IN ROOM _____

NUMBER _____

PART OF THE BODY _____

ADJECTIVE _____

ANIMAL (PLURAL) _____

VERB _____

NOUN _____

ADJECTIVE _____

ADJECTIVE _____

TYPE OF LIQUID _____

NOUN _____

ADJECTIVE _____

MAD LIBS®
LADIES AND GENTLEMEN,
THE GREAT GONZO!

Thank you, thank you! I am The Great Gonzo. In my time with the

Muppets, I have performed many __unhealthy__ acts. I have wrestled
                              ADJECTIVE

a/an __melty__ __Snowman__ while blindfolded. I have played
      ADJECTIVE   NOUN

that famous song by __Carter__ on the bagpipes while sitting atop
                    PERSON IN ROOM

a/an __448__-foot-tall flagpole. I've even recited the complete
      NUMBER

works of Shakespeare while suspended by my __heart__ above a
                                          PART OF THE BODY

pit of __jumpy__ and angry __pelicans__. (It would have
        ADJECTIVE   ANIMAL (PLURAL)

gone perfectly if I hadn't had to __run__ in the middle of it.)
                                  VERB

My courage, my creative vision, and my sheer lack of __Sheer__
                                                      NOUN

are without parallel. And while some have called me __Flat__,
                                                     ADJECTIVE

others have complimented me by calling me __bully__. But
                                           ADJECTIVE

when I succeed in balancing a flaming radial tire in a bathtub full of

__cranberry__ while reciting the lyrics to "Row, Row, Row Your
TYPE OF LIQUID

__quilt__," I feel like my life has meaning. I feel like a true and
NOUN

__crushed__ artist. That's why they call me The Great Gonzo!
ADJECTIVE

From THE MUPPETS MAD LIBS® • Copyright © 2016 Disney. Published by Price Stern Sloan, an imprint of
Penguin Random House LLC, 345 Hudson Street, New York, NY 10014.

MAD LIBS® is fun to play with friends, but you can also play it by yourself! To begin with, DO NOT look at the story on the page below. Fill in the blanks on this page with the words called for. Then, using the words you have selected, fill in the blank spaces in the story.

Now you've created your own hilarious MAD LIBS® game!

THE MUPPETS SOLVE A MYSTERY

NOUN _____

ADJECTIVE _____

A PLACE _____

VERB _____

ADJECTIVE _____

ADJECTIVE _____

OCCUPATION _____

A PLACE _____

VERB _____

NOUN _____

COLOR _____

MAD LIBS®
THE MUPPETS SOLVE A MYSTERY

Kermit the Frog and Fozzie Bear had just gotten jobs as reporters for

the *Daily* _____ when a thief made off with the expensive
               NOUN

jewels of a/an _____ fashion designer. Trying to get the
                ADJECTIVE

scoop, they flew to (the) _____ and, with the help of The
                          A PLACE

Great Gonzo, began an adventure known as "The Great Muppet

Caper." After finding a place to _____ at the shabby yet
                                   VERB

_____ Happiness Hotel, they were off to interview Lady
   ADJECTIVE

Holiday, the victim of the theft. At her office, they met a woman they

thought was Lady Holiday. Except the woman they interviewed wasn't

Lady Holiday at all! It was the one and only, _____ Miss
                                                ADJECTIVE

Piggy—Lady Holiday's personal _____. When another
                                OCCUPATION

necklace was stolen, the completely innocent Miss Piggy was framed

and thrown in (the) _____. But Gonzo overheard the thieves
                     A PLACE

plotting to _____ Lady Holiday's most prized jewel, the
             VERB

_____ Diamond! The Muppets realized that if they wanted
   NOUN

to rescue the gem and save Miss Piggy, they'd have to catch the thieves

_____-handed. Would they be able to save the day?
   COLOR

MAD LIBS® is fun to play with friends, but you can also play it by yourself! To begin with, DO NOT look at the story on the page below. Fill in the blanks on this page with the words called for. Then, using the words you have selected, fill in the blank spaces in the story.

Now you've created your own hilarious MAD LIBS® game!

DR. BUNSEN HONEYDEW AND BEAKER

NOUN _____

ADJECTIVE _____

NOUN _____

NOUN _____

ADJECTIVE _____

ADJECTIVE _____

ADJECTIVE _____

NOUN _____

VERB _____

ADVERB _____

NOUN _____

ADJECTIVE _____

ADJECTIVE _____

VERB ENDING IN "ING" _____

MAD LIBS®
DR. BUNSEN HONEYDEW
AND BEAKER

Good day! I am Dr. Bunsen Honeydew, and this is Muppet Labs, where

the future is being made today . . . and the _____ is being made
NOUN

tomorrow! We are so excited about our latest invention. What does

it do? Well, do you ever feel _____? Do you have problems
ADJECTIVE

with your _____? Now those worries can become a thing of
NOUN

the past with our brand-new Instant Automatic _____! My
NOUN

eager and _____ assistant, Beaker, will now demonstrate just
ADJECTIVE

how this _____ machine works. Won't you, Beaker? Come
ADJECTIVE

now, Beakie, don't be afraid—this technology is state of the art and

perfectly _____. Now, Beaker, we'll put this _____
ADJECTIVE   NOUN

on your head and I'll _____ the nozzle while we rotate these
VERB

dials _____ . . . Oh my, look at that smoke . . . and sparks . . .
ADVERB

and what a big, loud _____. It was quite an explosion! Beaker,
NOUN

I've never seen you looking so _____. This is a victory for
ADJECTIVE

science! Although, it looks rather _____ for you, Beakie . . .
ADJECTIVE

Beaker, stop _____! Where are you going? Oh well,
VERB ENDING IN "ING"

that's all for today from Muppet Labs. Isn't science wonderful?

MAD LIBS® is fun to play with friends, but you can also play it by yourself! To begin with, DO NOT look at the story on the page below. Fill in the blanks on this page with the words called for. Then, using the words you have selected, fill in the blank spaces in the story.

Now you've created your own hilarious MAD LIBS® game!

STATLER AND WALDORF

NUMBER _____

ADJECTIVE _____

ADJECTIVE _____

ADJECTIVE _____

NOUN _____

ADJECTIVE _____

PLURAL NOUN _____

ADJECTIVE _____

NOUN _____

TYPE OF FOOD (PLURAL) _____

MAD☺LIBS®

STATLER AND WALDORF

Statler: Why do these stories all have _____ words missing?
NUMBER

Waldorf: Beats me. But remember, we're talking about the _____
ADJECTIVE

Muppets. When have they ever done anything that made sense?

Statler: Good point. If you're looking for sense, don't try to get it from

the Muppets!

Waldorf: This book is so hard to read, it makes *War and Peace* look

like a/an _____ magazine.
ADJECTIVE

Statler: This book is so _____, it makes a/an _____
ADJECTIVE   NOUN

of knock-knock jokes look like *War and Peace*!

Waldorf: Why do they call this _____ thing Mad Libs?
ADJECTIVE

Statler: More like *Bad* Libs!

Waldorf: I'd rather eat live _____ than play this game!
PLURAL NOUN

Statler: There's one good thing I can say about this _____
ADJECTIVE

book . . .

Waldorf: What's that?

Statler: It makes a great _____!
NOUN

Waldorf: Ha! Say, let's go eat some _____. I'm starved!
TYPE OF FOOD (PLURAL)

MAD LIBS® is fun to play with friends, but you can also play it by yourself! To begin with, DO NOT look at the story on the page below. Fill in the blanks on this page with the words called for. Then, using the words you have selected, fill in the blank spaces in the story.

Now you've created your own hilarious MAD LIBS® game!

THE MUPPETS IN NEW YORK CITY

VERB _____

TYPE OF FOOD _____

ADJECTIVE _____

NOUN _____

NOUN _____

VERB _____

NOUN _____

ADJECTIVE _____

COLOR _____

NOUN _____

ADJECTIVE _____

ANIMAL (PLURAL) _____

MAD LIBS
THE MUPPETS IN NEW YORK CITY

Everybody knows the Muppets love to sing and _____. When
_____VERB

they put together a musical revue, people loved it so much that they

told the Muppets to take the show to the Big _____—New
_____TYPE OF FOOD

York City. So, Kermit the Frog and the rest of the Muppet gang visited

all the important and _____ Broadway producers, trying
_____ADJECTIVE

to find a/an _____ who would help them. Unfortunately,
_____NOUN

most threw the Muppets out the door and into the _____.
_____NOUN

After a while, the Muppets began to wonder if Kermit might be more

successful without them. So they left, pretending they had been hired

to _____ in other cities. Kermit missed his friends. They
_____VERB

meant more to him than _____. Finally, Kermit found
_____NOUN

a/an _____ Broadway producer who would put their show
_____ADJECTIVE

on "The Great _____ Way." It all looked great until Kermit
_____COLOR

lost his memory after an accident with a/an _____. All the
_____NOUN

Muppets had to work together to get the show up and running in time

for opening night. And the show was a/an _____ success,
_____ADJECTIVE

enjoyed by audiences and _____ alike.
_____ANIMAL (PLURAL)

MAD LIBS® is fun to play with friends, but you can also play it by yourself! To begin with, DO NOT look at the story on the page below. Fill in the blanks on this page with the words called for. Then, using the words you have selected, fill in the blank spaces in the story.

Now you've created your own hilarious MAD LIBS® game!

THE ELECTRIC MAYHEM

ADJECTIVE _____

NUMBER _____

VERB _____

ADJECTIVE _____

ADJECTIVE _____

NOUN _____

ADJECTIVE _____

ADJECTIVE _____

PART OF THE BODY _____

ADJECTIVE _____

COLOR _____

NOUN _____

ADJECTIVE _____

PLURAL NOUN _____

VERB _____

ADJECTIVE _____

PLURAL NOUN _____

NOUN _____

MAD LIBS®

THE ELECTRIC MAYHEM

The Electric Mayhem band has been playing _____ -style
                                             ADJECTIVE

music together for _____ years. Their lead singer, Dr. Teeth,
                      NUMBER

plays a mean keyboard and likes to _____ on the microphone.
                                         VERB

Janice plays lead guitar, shakes the tambourine, and wails as one of the

most _____ singers around. Sgt. Floyd Pepper rocks out on
        ADJECTIVE

the _____ bass and plays the vibes with lots of _____
      ADJECTIVE   NOUN

and soul. Zoot is the _____ saxophone player. He's always
                          ADJECTIVE

wearing his _____ fedora over his _____. Lips plays
                ADJECTIVE   PART OF THE BODY

the _____ trumpet and shakes his _____ hair like
      ADJECTIVE   COLOR

a wild _____. And of course, Animal is the _____
          NOUN   ADJECTIVE

drummer. He loves drums, _____, and rock and roll—and
                            PLURAL NOUN

bashing his drums like he wants to _____ them! The Electric
                                         VERB

Mayhem travels the world in their psychedelic bus. And when they

get to your _____ town, it's time to let your hair down, put
                ADJECTIVE

on your _____, and shake your groove _____ all
            PLURAL NOUN   NOUN

night long!

From THE MUPPETS MAD LIBS® • Copyright © 2016 Disney. Published by Price Stern Sloan, an imprint of
Penguin Random House LLC, 345 Hudson Street, New York, NY 10014.

MAD LIBS® is fun to play with friends, but you can also play it by yourself! To begin with, DO NOT look at the story on the page below. Fill in the blanks on this page with the words called for. Then, using the words you have selected, fill in the blank spaces in the story.

Now you've created your own hilarious MAD LIBS® game!

SCOOTER

NOUN _____

ADJECTIVE _____

NOUN _____

NUMBER _____

ADJECTIVE _____

NOUN _____

ADJECTIVE _____

A PLACE _____

PLURAL NOUN _____

NOUN _____

VERB _____

VERB _____

MAD LIBS

SCOOTER

A/An _____ about me? Gosh, I'd love to, but I don't have much
      NOUN

time now that I'm the talent coordinator/scout and associate producer

on *Up Late with Miss Piggy*. It's a big job. Every day brings a new,

_____ challenge! For instance, just today, Miss Piggy called me
ADJECTIVE

at 2:00 a.m. because she had a nightmare that someone called her a/an

_____, and I had to sing to her until she fell back to sleep. Today
NOUN

is a big day because we're filming a scene with a crowd of _____
                                                              NUMBER

extras. And as a very efficient and _____ talent coordinator/
                                       ADJECTIVE

scout and associate producer, I have to fill out paperwork for every

single one of them. I tried to get an early start, but Kermit the Frog, the

executive producer, showed up at the _____ of dawn. You know
                                          NOUN

how Kermit is—he's like the green, _____ glue that holds the
                                       ADJECTIVE

Muppets together. He sent me to the other side of (the) _____ to
                                                            A PLACE

pick up some _____ for Miss Piggy. Come to think of it, that's
                 PLURAL NOUN

exactly the kind of job I had to do when I was a/an _____.
                                                        NOUN

Well, no time to fret or _____, I promised Fozzie Bear I'd help
                            VERB

him _____ some new jokes. Gotta go!
        VERB

From THE MUPPETS MAD LIBS® • Copyright © 2016 Disney. Published by Price Stern Sloan, an imprint of
Penguin Random House LLC, 345 Hudson Street, New York, NY 10014.

MAD LIBS® is fun to play with friends, but you can also play it by yourself! To begin with, DO NOT look at the story on the page below. Fill in the blanks on this page with the words called for. Then, using the words you have selected, fill in the blank spaces in the story.

Now you've created your own hilarious MAD LIBS® game!

THE SWEDISH CHEF

NOUN _____

VERB ENDING IN "ING" _____

PLURAL NOUN _____

NOUN _____

VERB ENDING IN "ING" _____

PLURAL NOUN _____

TYPE OF FOOD _____

ADJECTIVE _____

VERB ENDING IN "ING" _____

ADJECTIVE _____

PLURAL NOUN _____

NOUN _____

ADJECTIVE _____

PART OF THE BODY _____

MAD LIBS®

THE SWEDISH CHEF

Have you ever met The Swedish Chef? Let's ask this a different way—

have you ever eaten exploding _____ shrimp? How about
_____NOUN_____

a soufflé that's so fluffy it goes _____ into the air?
_____VERB ENDING IN "ING"_____

Or a *ba-na-na-na-na-na-na* split that comes with its own dancing

_____? If you have, then you've probably enjoyed some
___PLURAL NOUN___

delicacies made by The Swedish Chef! From his floppy *toque blanche*

to the bristly _____ beneath his nose, The Swedish Chef is
_____NOUN_____

easy to recognize and impossible to understand. But whenever he's

_____ in the kitchen, you can tell he knows what
___VERB ENDING IN "ING"___

he's doing—even if no one else can figure it out. Why, you may ask,

is he always throwing _____ everywhere and putting
_____PLURAL NOUN_____

_____ in the skillet? The Swedish Chef might have some
___TYPE OF FOOD___

_____ ideas, like making doughnuts by _____
___ADJECTIVE___   ___VERB ENDING IN "ING"___

holes in _____ muffins, but he is always happy to share his
_____ADJECTIVE_____

culinary _____ with anybody who wants to watch. And
_____PLURAL NOUN_____

he's not afraid to sacrifice his own _____ for his recipes, even
_____NOUN_____

with sauce so _____ it blows his hat off his _____!
_____ADJECTIVE_____   ___PART OF THE BODY___

MAD LIBS® is fun to play with friends, but you can also play it by yourself! To begin with, DO NOT look at the story on the page below. Fill in the blanks on this page with the words called for. Then, using the words you have selected, fill in the blank spaces in the story.

Now you've created your own hilarious MAD LIBS® game!

ROWLF PLAYS THE BLUES

COLOR _____

NOUN _____

PART OF THE BODY _____

NOUN _____

NUMBER _____

NOUN _____

ADJECTIVE _____

NOUN _____

NOUN _____

A PLACE _____

NOUN _____

VERB _____

NOUN _____

SILLY WORD _____

VERB _____

ADJECTIVE _____

ADJECTIVE _____

MAD LIBS®

ROWLF PLAYS THE BLUES

Hi there, stranger. You look like you're feeling a little _____.
<u>COLOR</u>

Pull up a/an _____, sit down by my piano, and tell me the story
<u>NOUN</u>

of how you got your _____ broken. See, I can spot someone
<u>PART OF THE BODY</u>

who's pining for a lost _____ from _____ miles away.
<u>NOUN</u> <u>NUMBER</u>

When you've been tickling the ivories as long as I have, you've seen a

broken heart for every _____ of rain, and a/an _____
<u>NOUN</u> <u>ADJECTIVE</u>

dream for every falling star. I know that love can be one challenging

_____. That's why I stick to the single life. Every night when
<u>NOUN</u>

I finish work playing piano, I go home, read a/an _____, take
<u>NOUN</u>

myself for a walk, and go curl up in (the) _____. "Good dog,"
<u>A PLACE</u>

I tell myself. "Stay." Stay away from romance and flowers and songs

about _____. But, no matter how hard I _____, the
<u>NOUN</u> <u>VERB</u>

truth is that I can't stay away. I'm just like you—some bright new

_____ comes along, and before I know it, _____! I've
<u>NOUN</u> <u>SILLY WORD</u>

fallen in love once again. And all I can do is _____ the piano
<u>VERB</u>

and sing another _____ song about wonderful, beautiful,
<u>ADJECTIVE</u>

_____ love.
<u>ADJECTIVE</u>

MAD LIBS® is fun to play with friends, but you can also play it by yourself! To begin with, DO NOT look at the story on the page below. Fill in the blanks on this page with the words called for. Then, using the words you have selected, fill in the blank spaces in the story.

Now you've created your own hilarious MAD LIBS® game!

HOW THE MUPPETS REUNITED

ADJECTIVE _____

VERB (PAST TENSE) _____

PART OF THE BODY (PLURAL) _____

OCCUPATION _____

TYPE OF LIQUID _____

ADJECTIVE _____

NUMBER _____

ADJECTIVE _____

ADJECTIVE _____

ADJECTIVE _____

VERB _____

MAD LIBS
HOW THE MUPPETS
REUNITED

Walter is the most _____ Muppet fan who ever lived. His
                    ADJECTIVE

greatest dream was to visit Hollywood to see where his idols sang,

danced, and _____. When he finally got to go, he
            VERB (PAST TENSE)

couldn't believe his _____—Muppet Studios
                     PART OF THE BODY (PLURAL)

was in ruins. While wandering around, Walter overheard a rich

_____ who was going to buy the Muppet Theater to tear it
OCCUPATION

down to drill for _____! Walter couldn't let that happen.
                 TYPE OF LIQUID

So he found Kermit the Frog's house and explained to the world's

most _____ amphibian what was happening. The only
     ADJECTIVE

way to raise the _____ dollars they'd need to buy the Muppet
                 NUMBER

Theater back was to get all the Muppets back together and put on a/an

_____ show. It wasn't easy to convince everybody that getting
ADJECTIVE

back together was a/an _____ idea, but they did it for Kermit.
                      ADJECTIVE

And when the Muppets saw how much Walter loved and believed in

them, they knew they had to save the Muppet Theater—with a little

assistance from some very _____ celebrities who came to help
                          ADJECTIVE

_____ it for them.
VERB

MAD LIBS® is fun to play with friends, but you can also play it by yourself! To begin with, DO NOT look at the story on the page below. Fill in the blanks on this page with the words called for. Then, using the words you have selected, fill in the blank spaces in the story.

Now you've created your own hilarious MAD LIBS® game!

UNCLE DEADLY

ADJECTIVE _____

PERSON IN ROOM _____

COLOR _____

ADJECTIVE _____

NUMBER _____

ADJECTIVE _____

NOUN _____

NOUN _____

ADJECTIVE _____

ADJECTIVE _____

ADJECTIVE _____

VERB ENDING IN "ING" _____

MAD LIBS®

UNCLE DEADLY

"Mad" Libs, you say? How fascinating. In my _____ days
                                                ADJECTIVE

performing at the Muppet Theater, I played quite a few mad characters—

Hamlet, _____, and of course Othello. It was while playing
         PERSON IN ROOM

this last Shakespearean classic, possessed by the _____-eyed
                                                        COLOR

monster of jealousy, that I met my untimely demise at the hands of

the _____ critics. I spent the next _____ years haunting
       ADJECTIVE   NUMBER

various _____ venues beside some of the greatest spirits of our
         ADJECTIVE

time, such as the Ghost of _____ Past and the _____ of
                             NOUN   NOUN

the Opera. But, after my ill-advised effort at being a villain with an oil

magnate and a/an _____ bear named Bobo, I discovered I'm
                    ADJECTIVE

truly a/an _____ creature at heart. Who says you can't turn
             ADJECTIVE

over a new leaf, or at least rake it into a surprisingly _____
                                                              ADJECTIVE

pile? The Muppets have embraced me as one of their own, and I now

spend my days as wardrobe supervisor on *Up Late with Miss Piggy*,

_____ Miss Piggy look her best.
VERB ENDING IN "ING"

From THE MUPPETS MAD LIBS® • Copyright © 2016 Disney. Published by Price Stern Sloan, an imprint of
Penguin Random House LLC, 345 Hudson Street, New York, NY 10014.

MAD LIBS® is fun to play with friends, but you can also play it by yourself! To begin with, DO NOT look at the story on the page below. Fill in the blanks on this page with the words called for. Then, using the words you have selected, fill in the blank spaces in the story.

Now you've created your own hilarious MAD LIBS® game!

CONSTANTINE: KERMIT'S EVIL LOOK-ALIKE

NOUN _____

ADJECTIVE _____

NOUN _____

NOUN _____

A PLACE _____

NOUN _____

ADJECTIVE _____

A PLACE _____

VERB ENDING IN "ING" _____

NOUN _____

NOUN _____

ADJECTIVE _____

ADJECTIVE _____

After the Muppets reunited, they decided to take their act on the

road. They found a manager named Dominic Badguy who seemed

like a very trustworthy _____. Little did the Muppets know,
                         NOUN

he was working for Constantine, the world's most _____
                                                  ADJECTIVE

criminal. Constantine looked exactly like Kermit the Frog except

for a/an _____ on his face—and he had a plan to use the
          NOUN

Muppets to pull off a major _____ heist. At the first stop
                             NOUN

on their tour, in (the) _____, Constantine kidnapped Kermit,
                         A PLACE

glued a/an _____ on his face, and threw him in the street.
            NOUN

Because he looked like Constantine, our hero was arrested and sent

to the most _____ prison in (the) _____. Meanwhile,
             ADJECTIVE   A PLACE

Constantine pretended to be Kermit by singing and dancing and

_____. He even wooed Miss Piggy by giving her
VERB ENDING IN "ING"

everything she wanted, including a/an _____. Would anybody
                                       NOUN

notice that "Kermit" was a/an _____? Or would our brave
                               NOUN

and _____ hero be stuck in the _____ prison forever?
     ADJECTIVE   ADJECTIVE

MAD LIBS® is fun to play with friends, but you can also play it by yourself! To begin with, DO NOT look at the story on the page below. Fill in the blanks on this page with the words called for. Then, using the words you have selected, fill in the blank spaces in the story.

Now you've created your own hilarious MAD LIBS® game!

SAM EAGLE

ADJECTIVE _____

NOUN _____

ADVERB _____

NOUN _____

PERSON IN ROOM _____

VERB ENDING IN "ING" _____

ADJECTIVE _____

NOUN _____

PLURAL NOUN _____

NOUN _____

VERB ENDING IN "ING" _____

PLURAL NOUN _____

ADJECTIVE _____

ADJECTIVE _____

VERB ENDING IN "ING" _____

MAD LIBS

SAM EAGLE

Stop! I would like to say a few words about this _____
                                                    ADJECTIVE

book of so-called Muppet "Mad" Libs. My job is to make sure that

every _____ the Muppets participate in is morally upright,
        NOUN

_____ wholesome, and free of unpatriotic _____.
   ADVERB   NOUN

(Frankly, it's not an easy job. I wouldn't even wish it on _____.)
                                                            PERSON IN ROOM

I, for one, am appalled by the idea of _____ around
                                         VERB ENDING IN "ING"

with the English language and turning the creative act of _____
                                                            ADJECTIVE

writing into some kind of game. The English language is not some silly

_____! What is the socially redeeming value in leaving out all
   NOUN

these words and replacing them with any kind of _____?
                                                   PLURAL NOUN

Must we all sound like a/an _____ of weirdos? What's next—
                              NOUN

will we start _____ pure gibberish? Someone must
                VERB ENDING IN "ING"

work for integrity and _____. Unfortunately, the only one
                         PLURAL NOUN

willing to do this thankless and _____ job is me. Please, join
                                   ADJECTIVE

me in stamping out this _____ nonsense once and for all! Stop
                          ADJECTIVE

_____ this book immediately!
   VERB ENDING IN "ING"

MAD LIBS® is fun to play with friends, but you can also play it by yourself! To begin with, DO NOT look at the story on the page below. Fill in the blanks on this page with the words called for. Then, using the words you have selected, fill in the blank spaces in the story.

Now you've created your own hilarious MAD LIBS® game!

A ROUGH DAY FOR KERMIT THE FROG

ADJECTIVE _____

ADVERB _____

CELEBRITY _____

VERB ENDING IN "ING" _____

NUMBER _____

PLURAL NOUN _____

ADVERB _____

ADJECTIVE _____

NOUN _____

ADJECTIVE _____

PLURAL NOUN _____

PLURAL NOUN _____

Being the executive producer of the talk show *Up Late with Miss Piggy* can be a/an _____ job. Today, Kermit the Frog's morning
_____ADJECTIVE_____

started with _____ bad news: _____, who was supposed
_____ADVERB_____ _____CELEBRITY_____

to be on the show, had to cancel due to a/an _____
_____VERB ENDING IN "ING"_____

accident. Kermit tried to get _____ minutes alone with the host,
_____NUMBER_____

Miss Piggy, but Fozzie Bear kept interrupting to ask for his opinion

on a few new jokes. When Miss Piggy finally arrived, she stomped

through the office, throwing _____, and complaining
_____PLURAL NOUN_____

_____ to Kermit that the lighting in her dressing room was too
_____ADVERB_____

_____. Kermit tried to find Scooter to help, but Scooter was
_____ADJECTIVE_____

already busy helping The Electric Mayhem fix their set after Animal

threw a/an _____ during band practice. Kermit hid in his
_____NOUN_____

office and wondered if he should run away to a peaceful swamp where

the days are _____ and they have all the _____
_____ADJECTIVE_____ _____PLURAL NOUN_____

you can eat. But, like the professional he is, Kermit pulled himself up

by his _____, stepped out of his office, and declared, "It's
_____PLURAL NOUN_____

time to get things started!"

MAD LIBS® is fun to play with friends, but you can also play it by yourself! To begin with, DO NOT look at the story on the page below. Fill in the blanks on this page with the words called for. Then, using the words you have selected, fill in the blank spaces in the story.

Now you've created your own hilarious MAD LIBS® game!

MISS PIGGY'S GUIDE TO BEING FABULOUS

PLURAL NOUN _____

NOUN _____

ADJECTIVE _____

PLURAL NOUN _____

VERB _____

ADJECTIVE _____

CELEBRITY (FEMALE) _____

VERB _____

ADVERB _____

TYPE OF FOOD _____

OCCUPATION _____

TYPE OF LIQUID _____

SILLY WORD _____

VERB _____

ADJECTIVE _____

ADJECTIVE _____

MAD LIBS®
MISS PIGGY'S GUIDE TO BEING FABULOUS

Listen up, all my dear _____, because the beauty secrets
                                PLURAL NOUN

I am about to reveal are priceless! Your personal style is like your

_____; Either you have it or you don't. Take *moi*; ever
     NOUN

since I was a young and extremely _____ girl, I knew what
                                      ADJECTIVE

kind of _____ to wear and how to _____ my
          PLURAL NOUN   VERB

hair. And now that I am the world's most _____ star, I am
                                              ADJECTIVE

known as a style icon, much like _____, only with
                                  CELEBRITY (FEMALE)

far more talent. If you want to _____ like me, you have to be
                                    VERB

like me. How is this possible? When I wake up in the morning and

emerge _____ from my boudoir, the very first thing I do is
         ADVERB

nourish my skin by eating a big bowl of _____. Next, I have
                                          TYPE OF FOOD

a professional _____ style my hair while I am reclining in a
                 OCCUPATION

bath of _____. Next, my personal dresser, Uncle Deadly,
         TYPE OF LIQUID

helps me select my clothes using an ancient method he brought over

from _____-vania. And voilà, I'm ready to _____
       SILLY WORD   VERB

the day! Can you look as _____ as *moi*? Probably not, but
                          ADJECTIVE

following my _____ advice can't hurt. *N'est-ce pas?*
              ADJECTIVE

MAD LIBS® is fun to play with friends, but you can also play it by yourself! To begin with, DO NOT look at the story on the page below. Fill in the blanks on this page with the words called for. Then, using the words you have selected, fill in the blank spaces in the story.

Now you've created your own hilarious MAD LIBS® game!

STATLER AND WALDORF (AGAIN)

VERB _____

ADJECTIVE _____

PLURAL NOUN _____

ADJECTIVE _____

ADJECTIVE _____

VERB _____

ADJECTIVE _____

A PLACE _____

ADJECTIVE _____

ADVERB _____

Statler: That's it? It's over?

Waldorf: Finally. I thought they'd never _____!

VERB

Statler: What kind of a/an _____ book was that? It didn't

ADJECTIVE

have a story, characters, or _____.

PLURAL NOUN

Waldorf: Worse than that, it had those _____ Muppets.

ADJECTIVE

Statler: What did you think of the stories about Kermit the Frog?

Waldorf: I didn't think of them at all! How about that _____

ADJECTIVE

bear, Fozzie?

Statler: He made me so happy I could _____.

VERB

Waldorf: Really? When was that?

Statler: When he went away!

Waldorf: I wish he'd gone away before page one!

Statler: This _____ book really moved me.

ADJECTIVE

Waldorf: Yeah, it made me want to move to (the) _____.

A PLACE

Statler: There is one good thing about this _____ book.

ADJECTIVE

Waldorf: What's that?

Statler: It's _____ over!

ADVERB

Download Mad Libs today!

Join the millions of Mad Libs fans creating
wacky and wonderful stories on our apps!